C. P. Snow

by WILLIAM COOPER

by Longmans, Green & Co.
and the National Book League
Published for the British Council

Three shillings and sixpence net

'C. P. Snow is a novelist of unique experience'. Mr. Cooper opens his study with these words, and he proves them to be true by a careful, critical analysis, in particular of that remarkable and continuing sequence, *Strangers And Brothers*.

Snow's uniqueness consists of his deep experience of several distinct worlds—that of the scientist, that of Government, that of the universities, and that of the artist and student of humanity. This experience he has blended in his novels, and it is Mr. Cooper's purpose to show the very special value, to our own times and to the future, of what Snow has written. This sympathetic interpretation enables the reader to achieve a deeper insight into a man of singularly varied gifts.

William Cooper is himself one of the most distinguished novelists to emerge since the war. *Scenes from Provincial Life* is a novel which has had a seminal effect on the succeeding generation of novelists.

Bibliographical Series

of Supplements to 'British Book News'
on Writers and Their Work

★

GENERAL EDITOR
Bonamy Dobrée

C. P. SNOW
from a photograph by WALTER BIRD

C. P. SNOW

by

WILLIAM COOPER

PUBLISHED FOR
THE BRITISH COUNCIL
and the NATIONAL BOOK LEAGUE
by LONGMANS, GREEN & CO.

LONGMANS, GREEN & CO. LTD.,
48 Grosvenor Street, London, W.1.
Railway Crescent, Croydon, Victoria, Australia
Auckland, Kingston (Jamaica), Lahore, Nairobi

LONGMANS SOUTHERN AFRICA (PTY) LTD.
Thibault House, Thibault Square, Cape Town,
Johannesburg, Salisbury

LONGMANS OF NIGERIA LTD.
W.R. Industrial Estate, Ikeja

LONGMANS OF GHANA LTD.
Industrial Estate, Ring Road South, Accra

LONGMANS GREEN (FAR EAST) LTD.
443 Lockhart Road, Hong Kong

LONGMANS OF MALAYA LTD.
44 Jalan Ampang, Kuala Lumpur

ORIENT LONGMANS LTD.
Calcutta, Bombay, Madras
Delhi, Hyderabad, Dacca

LONGMANS CANADA LTD.
137 Bond Street, Toronto 2

Printed in Great Britain by
F. Mildner & Sons, London, E.C.1

Contents

Born 15 October 1905, Leicester: son of William Edward Snow, F.R.C.O., and Ada Sophia.

1925 Entered University College, Leicester.

1927 Graduated B.Sc. First Class Honours.

1928 M.Sc. Entered Christ's College, Cambridge as a Research Student.

1930 Senior Studentship of the 1851 Exhibition: elected a Fellow of Christ's College.

1932 *Death Under Sail.*

1933 *New Lives For Old.*

1934 *The Search.*

1935 Appointed Tutor of Christ's College.

1939 Appointed to Royal Society Sub-Committee on use of scientific personnel.

1940 Joined Ministry of Labour. *Strangers And Brothers.*

1942 Director of Technical Personnel, Ministry of Labour.

1943 C.B.E.

1944 Director of Scientific Personnel, English Electric Company.

1945 Civil Service Commissioner.

1947 Director of English Electric Company. *The Light And The Dark.*

1949 *Time of Hope.*

1950 Married Pamela Hansford Johnson. *View Over The Park*, a play, produced at Lyric Theatre, Hammersmith.

1951 *The Masters.*

1952 Son, Philip Charles Hansford, born.

1954 *The New Men.*

1956 *Homecomings.*

1957 Knighted.

1958 *The Conscience Of The Rich.*

1959 Rede Lecturer, Cambridge.

1960 Retired from Civil Service. *The Affair.*

1961 Godkin Lecturer, Harvard. Dramatisation of *The Affair* produced at Strand Theatre.

1962 Rector of St. Andrews: Inaugural Address.

C. P. SNOW

I

BIOGRAPHY

C. P. SNOW is a novelist of unique expereience. At a period of history when the worlds of literature, and of science and technology, are sharply separated from each other, he has come to hold a key-position in both simultaneously. A novelist by vocation, he is also a scientific administrator and man of affairs.

Snow was born in 1905, the second of four sons in a lower middle-class family living in Leicester. The city, whose existence is based on the hosiery and boot-and-shoe trades, has always been relatively prosperous: the family—his father had a minor job in a boot-and-shoe firm—was relatively unprosperous. The effect of such a situation on an intelligent and affectionate young boy is touchingly described at the beginning of his novel *Time Of Hope* (1949). Nevertheless Snow's was a family strongly rooted in a stable, flourishing part of industrialised society; and consequently Snow's tone when writing about society, both the part of it in which he was born and the parts which he has got to know later, has always been deep-seatedly confident.

He was educated as a scientist. He went to Alderman Newton's Grammar School, where, at the stage of entering the Sixth Form, he specialised in science. As the school at that time had no Arts Sixth, he had no option; though he says now that, when committing himself to a career to which he was not unequivocally drawn, he thought that he would be able to 'break through' later to what he really wanted to do.

After leaving the school, Snow returned there as a laboratory assistant while working for a university scholarship. In those days it was much less easy than it is nowadays to get a free university education. He won a scholarship which took him to Leicester University College—whose students took London degrees—where he got a First Class Honours in chemistry of such brilliance that he was awarded a grant to stay on and do research. He chose to work in the field of infra-red spectroscopy, which attracted him because of its susceptibility to theoretical study in terms of the currently developing quantum mechanics. He took an M.Sc. in physics in 1928 and was awarded a scholarship which enabled him to go up to Cambridge, where he entered Christ's College as a research student.

At Cambridge the quality of his research was such that in 1930 his College elected him to a Fellowship, which meant that he might hope to find a permanent place in a university: among scientists he was beginning to be spoken of, like Arthur Miles in *The Search*, as a bright young man. His future career in scientific research looked as though it were settled. In the last few years, however, he had grown more certain, rather than less, that his future career lay elsewhere; so he turned to literature. He had begun to think of 'breaking through'. He writes:

'I was educated as a scientist, as Miles was: but I never had his single-minded passion, and in fact knew my own ultimate vocation from the time I was about eighteen'. Prefatory Note to re-issue of *The Search* (1958).

The ultimate vocation he knew as his own was that of a novelist. As a beginning he wrote two novels, a detective story and a Wellsian work of scientific imagination. They served the dual purpose of enabling him to get his hand in as a writer, and, because they were in an easily recognisable, uncontroversial mode, of getting him ready publication.

In 1933 he came to a turning-point. It is impossible to sustain simultaneously a career as a research scientist and a career as a novelist. Original research and creative art both draw on the same source of physic energy. Though they may exist together for a time, in the end one of them has to go. Snow's turning-point, a piece of research that went wrong through oversight, was externally rather like that in Arthur Miles's scientific career, though different, of course, internally. Snow went away and wrote *The Search*, his first serious novel. In effect, the 'break through' was complete. From then on he did no more research. However, he continued to teach science in the university, and was appointed to a college Tutorship in 1934.

Yet *The Search*, though it made a reputation for Snow as a novelist, did not represent what he finally meant to write. In his Prefatory Note to the 1958 edition of *The Search* he says: 'It was a false start. I wanted to say something about people first and foremost, and then people-on-society, in a quite different way, and at a quite different level from anything in this book'.

On 1 January, 1935, Snow had the original idea—he records that the idea was quite sharp—for the chain of novels, which is commonly known as the Lewis Eliot series, and which has finally been given the title borne by the first book in the series, *Strangers And Brothers*. It is clear now that whereas *The Search* was a study of individual character against a background of society, *Strangers And Brothers* is a study, at once more penetrating and more revealing, of individual character acting upon society and reacting to it. By 1939 Snow had laid down the general pattern of the series and had written the first volume. Then war broke out. He put writing aside, and did not resume until 1945.

During the autumn of 1939, Snow had been asked by a committee of the Royal Society to assist in devising the best way of organising university scientists for the war. In 1940 the function of this committee was formally taken over by the Ministry of Labour, and Snow became a civil servant. He was thus brought into public affairs. During the war his chief rôle was to exercise personal judgement on how individual scientists might be best employed, in research, in government research establishments or industry, or as technical officers in the Armed Forces; and to plan how the number of scientists and engineers in the country might be increased. In the course of this work he formed a friendship with the Chairman of the English Electric Company, which led to his being invited in 1944 to act as personnel adviser to the firm, and in 1947 to join the Board of Directors.

When the war was over Snow was invited to become a Civil Service Commissioner with special responsibility for scientific appointments. Although this represented a change from acting as an employment agency to acting as an employer, the same techniques of human and scientific judgement were required—assisted, in Snow's case, by a wide-ranging interest in scientific and engineering research, together with a remarkable memory for the professional records of individual scientists. Since he was now free to start writing novels again, he accepted only a part-time appointment. For all his activities in public affairs and industry, he intended to make certain of reserving some of his time for his creative work.

Snow's rôle in affairs from 1945 was considerable, yet not easy to define. He participated in all the major appointments of scientists to the government service; and he acted as an essential point of reference in questions of official policy relating to scientific man-power and technological education. But one may presume that his major contribution, less formal and more permeating, was to bridge the gap between scientists, whose professional training tends not to encourage them in making human judgements, and men of affairs, whose professional training may leave them someting short of adequate when making scientific judgements. For his services to the country in public affairs a knighthood was conferred on him in 1957. However the time came when he felt he must free himself altogether from his formal commitments to official life, and in 1960 he retired from the Civil Service.

Since 1947, Snow has published seven more novels of the projected eleven which will complete the *Strangers And Brothers* cycle. It is quite different from a chronicle-sequence, or a *roman fleuve*. In content it is essentially a personal story —the story of a man's life, through which is revealed his psychological and his moral structure—yet by extension and implication it is an enquiry into the psychological and moral structure of a large fraction of the society of our times. As further volumes appear its form is disclosed as massive and intricate, yet fundamentally simple. And in concept it has been seminal: several other serious writers have more recently taken up this kind of novel-cycle as an essential form.[1] *Strangers And Brothers* must inevitably be regarded as a key-work of the decades in which it was written.

In addition to his two main activities as novelist and administrator, Snow has many others, public and private. He married Pamela Hansford Johnson, the novelist, in 1950, and they have a son. He writes for English and American journals and periodicals, chiefly on the theme for which his unique position in the literary and scientific worlds specially fits him. Seeing the literary and the scientific worlds becoming even more sharply separated, he devotes himself to the task of bringing them together. This is one of the activities in which he is coming to influence current thought about the nature and future of our culture.

[1] Examples of interest are Mr. Anthony Powell's *The Music Of Time*, and Mrs. Doris Lessing's *Martha Quest* series.

II

EARLY NOVELS

Death Under Sail (1932) was Snow's first novel. It is a detective story, about a murder on a sailing-boat in the middle of the Norfolk Broads: it conforms to the conventions, and the plot is admirably organised. But what singles it out from other novels in the *genre* is the fact that the plot grows out of the characters rather than the characters out of the plot. They are presented as interesting persons outside the puzzle; and though the author treats them with uncommon psychological understanding, something is always left, as it would be in a serious novel, for the reader's speculation.

It is, of course, very much a young man's book and very much of the early 30's—it sparkles with high spirits, and the importance of *l'amour* and sophistication are taken with delightful romantic gravity—and yet the sureness of his style and, even more notably, the sureness of his literary tact, signalise a writer who, having decided what he intended to do, has exactly done it. *Death Under Sail* was an odd but nevertheless remarkable beginning.

New Lives For Old (1933) was published anonymously. It is about the discovery of a hormone which will effect the rejuvenation of human beings, and the time is what was then the future—the story begins in about 1950 and ends just over thirty years later. The consequences of the discovery are the moral and economic deterioration of the western world.

At the time Snow was doing research, and among scientists was being spoken of as a bright young man: it seemed possible that the publication of this book might lead to his being spoken of as too bright. *Death Under Sail* had not done any damage of this kind, possibly because the majority of scientists (*a*) did not take detective stories seriously, and (*b*) liked reading them in their spare time.

Actually it can now be seen that publication of *New Lives For Old* under his own name would not have made any difference to Snow's career.

New Lives For Old is inferior to Wells's early achievements in this *genre*. It opens, as they do, in matter-of-fact realism; but remains there, with no touch of that Wellsian inflation of manner necessary to bring off such a story completely. Also, where Wells was writing out of unalloyed optimism, Snow's vision was darker, and his psychological insight, especially into the sexual natures of men and women, too disturbingly truthful to find a comfortable place in fantasicated history.

Incidentally the book contains an interesting reference to 'consciousness', which was pre-occupying Snow during that period, '. . . consciousness of motive, awareness of one's emotions and those of the people around one, perception of the reasons behind the actions that human beings do'. It is this particular pre-occupation that is the clue to the investigatory element in all Snow's later novels.

The Search (1934) was the first novel Snow wrote outside a specific *genre*. It is the story of a young scientist, Arthur Miles, told in the first person, from his boyhood to maturity: he makes his way, by means of scholarships, from lower middle-class origins to a position of distinction in the scientific world.[1] *The Search* is the only novel about being a scientist to be written by a man who, at the time of writing, was more distinguished as a scientist than as a novelist; and it gives the most authentic answers to some of the questions that pre-occupy most non-scientists a quarter of a century later—What is it like to be a scientist? What is it like to do experiments, to make a discovery?

The Search also illuminates the question of whether the pursuit of scientific truth and the pursuit of a career in science conflict or accord with each other, or can be, in the

[1] The extent to which *The Search* is autobiographical is commented upon by the author in the Prefatory Note to the re-issue of the novel in 1958.

end, the same thing. Arthur Miles, at the height of early
success in research, becomes involved in the 'politics' of
getting a research institute founded; and while so doing,
overlooks an important detail in the current research on
which his reputation depends. His career as a scientist
collapses, and he is forced to ask himself the most searching
questions of all.

The main point about the novel, however, is that it
creates for the reader not 'a scientist', but a whole individual
who happens to be a scientist. And instead of handing the
reader the answers to his questions, it enables him, by
putting him in possession of the whole individual, to
disentangle the answers—if they exist—for himself.

III

THE SEQUENCE, STRANGERS AND BROTHERS

Massive and intricate, the novel-sequence *Strangers And Brothers* is fundamentally simple in design. It traces the life-story of the narrator, Lewis Eliot, in terms of alternation between what Snow himself calls 'direct experience' and observed experience'. The titles of the novels in the sequence that have been published so far can be set out on the page to illustrate this:

Strangers And Brothers 1925-33
The Conscience Of The Rich 1927-36

Time Of Hope 1914-33

The Light And The Dark 1935-43
The Masters 1937
The New Men 1939-46

Homecomings 1938-48

The Affair 1953-54

The books in the column on the left are those in which Lewis Eliot, in the rôle more of observer than participant,[1] tells the stories of his friends: they are predominantly 'observed experience'. In those on the right Lewis Eliot tells his own story: they are predominantly 'direct experience'.[2]

The dates following the title of a novel are those of the period in time which the novel covers. The first three novels form a cycle in which Lewis tells first the story of two of his friends, and then his own story over the same period. Then follows a second, similar cycle; and *The Affair* is the beginning of a third and last.

Each novel, though its place in the sequence is clear, is designed so that it can stand alone, a self-contained story

[1] There is a resemblance, in this rôle, to that of Henry James's 'foreground observer'.

[2] Predominantly—for a novelist completely to segregate observed and direct experience is scarcely possible; and if he did succeed in doing so, the result would seem peculiarly sterile.

which anyone can fully understand without having read any of the other books. Yet each book gains, as Snow, in planning the series intended that each book might gain, by being read in conjunction with the books that precede it—and that follow it. *Strangers And Brothers* is based on the concept that the present moment of time is indissolubly a part of the past and of the future: it can be taken on its own, complete as it is in itself; but only when it is shown to have embedded in it signs of what has gone before, and what is to come, does it signify fully.

Strangers And Brothers (1940) is about George Passant, twenty-six years old and six years Lewis's senior, a qualified clerk in the most solid firm of solicitors in Lewis's native provincial town, who in the mid-1920's gives evening lectures on law at the local Institute of Arts and Technology, which Lewis formerly attended; and who, by force of his personality, is the focus of a group of young people who look to him for guidance in both their careers and their lives. These are far from the 1920's of popular conception in the 1950's—whimsical, riotous, modishly decadent. For George's friends in the provinces they are years of hard work and hard, dazzling hopes.

The story of George Passant is tragic, tragic in its sense of human loss. He is a remarkable man, gifted with formidable intelligence and striking personality, a man of probity, integrity and loyalty. He has the makings of a great man. At the end of the novel, in 1933, he is seen escaping by the skin of his teeth from the criminal charge of fraud, squalid, petty fraud. How could it have happened? Where was the flaw?

George Passant is an idealist, with the idealist's capacity for creating a private world, a cosmos, from his own fantasies. The elements on which his cosmos is founded are freedom and hope. Living among what Lewis calls 'the ragtag and bobtail of the lower middle-classes', he has gathered round him young people of promise, to whom he means to bring freedom from constraining habits and

conventions of thought, and hope for wider horizons and
more brilliant careers. 'The world seemed on the march',
says Lewis. 'We wanted to join in.' George translates his
cosmos into a reality. He welds his young people into a
group which migrates at week-ends to an isolated farm on
the outskirts of the town, to experience there a foretaste,
or perhaps only a simulacrum, of the intellectual and social
freedom that he desires for them. In the group are some
attractive girls.

Now George Passant has a strongly sensual nature. At
first his sensuality is completely separated from his idealism.
But then there comes into his group a very different kind
of young man, Jack Cotery, dashing and engaging, labile,
something of an amorist. Jack is morally blind; and he
goes straight to the core of moral blindness in George—
for George, despite his stature of mind and of personality,
is vulnerable to his own desires: just as his idealistic cosmos
cuts him off from the world of ordinary men, so this blindness cuts him off from true perception of his own motives.
Jack Cotery's world of ordinary men happens to operate
on the edge of sharp practice: his insight into George's
motives is artlessly cynical.

Strangers And Brothers begins with a trivial scandal in
which George saves Jack Cotery from a minor misfortune:
it ends with a major scandal in which George, as a result of
Jack's activities, stands in danger of utter ruin.

For two reasons this novel may be felt to be the most
'difficult' of the sequence. The first reason is the psychological rarity of George Passant himself: the reader may
find himself without previous experience of anyone like
him. (On the other hand, though George is far removed
from the author in temperament, he is the most triumphantly realised character in the sequence.) The other
reason is that in meeting the analytical problem, Snow has
left the book rather bare of those familiar incidentals that
help the reader along. Even so, the book has an extraordinary
atmosphere, pervading, almost claustrophobic. For this,

and above all for sheer originality of theme, *Strangers And Brothers* has a claim to be regarded as the most remarkable novel of the entire sequence to date.

The Conscience Of The Rich comes second in the sequence, although it was not published till 1958. It is about Lewis's friend, Charles March. It begins in London, in 1927, when Charles and Lewis, about the same age, are pupils at the Bar, though they have entered different chambers. Lewis, who is attracted to Charles as much by his warmth of heart, his patience and his delicacy of feeling as by his incisive mind, is astonished by the cold, angry voice in which Charles invites him to his house. He soon discovers the meaning of it: the invitation has forced Charles to disclose that he is the son of a rich, aristocratic anglo-Jewish family. And Charles suffers from conflicting emotions about being Jewish and about being rich.

Lewis is introduced to Mr. March, Charles's father, an active, lively man, comically fluid in change of mood, yet essentially pertinacious, who retired at the age of thirty-three from competitive existence as owner of the family bank, and who now lives, with undisguised pleasure and apprehension, entirely for his children. 'I want something for you', he says to Charles. 'I wish I could know that you'll get something that I've always wanted for you'. Even so early in the story, Lewis foresees that though Charles may arrive at some sort of harmony with his own Jewish origins, he can only arrive at tragic disharmony with his father; for in the depths of his nature, Charles is equally self-centred.

Possessive love is the principal theme of this novel, though there are several others. Charles is forbidden by his conscience to take advantage of the opportunities given him by his wealth. He might easily become an adornment to fashionable society, equally easily carve out a brilliant personal success at the Bar with the help of his family connections. He will do neither. After a violent quarrel with

his father, who retaliates by trying to keep him financially
dependent, he embarks, humbly, like any poverty-stricken
student, on training for the medical profession—a profession
which promises him only that he will be *useful* to the human
beings about him.

In this revolt, he has the encouragement of Ann Jessel,
the girl he is going to marry. Unlike the man whom
Charles's sister, Katherine, marries, causing Mr. March
further misery, Ann is both Jewish and moderately rich.
She, however, is suffering a conflict of conscience parallel
to Charles's: like many non-Jewish rich young men and
women of her time, she is in revolt against the disastrous
trend of history which her own class appears to her to be
accelerating, and she has become a Communist. At the end
of the book she finds herself in a position to wreck the career
of Mr. March's most beloved and revered elder brother.

There is no chance of Charles and his father ever coming
to terms. The possessive love of parents for children is
'a darkness of the heart'. Yet, like George Passant, in the
preceding novel, the two men, in the midst of their suffering, are strengthened by hope, hope for the future.

Time Of Hope (1949) is the first novel of 'direct experience'. Lewis Eliot now tells his own life-story, beginning in
1914, when he was nine years old, and ending in 1933,
shortly after George Passant's trial and just before Charles
March's marriage.

While being a novel of self-revelation, *Time Of Hope* is,
more subtly, a novel of self-discovery. In telling the story
of George Passant, Lewis sees a man whose potentialities
are brought to nothing by a peculiarity of nature so intrinsic
as to be irremediable—even by the effort of intelligence and
will. Telling the story of his own life, Lewis discovers a
different kind of flaw, a particular strand in his nature which,
apart from whether it is responsible for causing him
unhappiness or not, affronts his moral apprehensions.
Brought near to failure in his career, after a brilliant start,
and brought to ruin in his marriage, through his own

choice, he finds himself, in self-discovery, stating the nature of a moral struggle which he intends shall occupy the next part of his life. Intelligence and will in this struggle *can* avail. There *is* hope.

It is in love, which Lewis sees as the profoundest relationship between human beings, that he discovers himself. First in his love for his mother, and then in his love for his wife, he realises that there is something gravely wrong from his side. His mother, vain and imperious, yet passionately anxious for his future success in life, loves him without restraint—and he is unable to respond equally. The possessiveness of her love provokes him to evasion: when her emotions flow towards him, he absents himself. She dies without his being able to tell her that his own ambitions match her dreams for him.

After his mother's death, his ambitions flare up beyond anything his friends had expected of him. From a clerking job in a local government office, he decides to work for the Bar. And he begins with remarkable success. He is a very clever young man and outward-turning by nature: he makes many friends, for he is affectionate and sympathetic —provided his innermost reserve is not menaced, he can respond with emotion more freely-flowing than most men's. And in his detachment he has a knack for handling other men shrewdly. Yet, by the time he is twenty-eight, and practising at the Bar, he knows that, judged by the standard of his talents and his first ambitions, he has not come off. His career has been eroded by his marriage.

For eight years Lewis has been in love with a girl called Sheila Knight. She has the gift of beauty. And she is incapable of sustained feeling. In the depths of her nature she is remote and splintered, so that her emotions seem to arise, jerkily and fleetingly, from un-connected sources. In desperation, for the sake of making herself feel at all, she turns cruelly on anyone who is devoted to her. Having failed to love, she lets Lewis marry her. Now, for the first time, Lewis is not evading, absenting himself. His innermost reserve is thrown open to another human being, to another human being who can neither give nor demand anything in return. He loves her without restraint *because* she can neither give nor demand anything in return. And so he discovers what is wrong with him. The bar to his innermost reserve is vanity, vanity so strong that it can be broken down not by another's love but only by his own suffering.

As *Time Of Hope* ends, the central problem for Lewis Eliot is at last stated. He has discovered what is wrong, and that, in itself, gives him some hope. He also knows what he must do, if he is ever going to have the profoundest relationship with another human being.

The Light And The Dark (1947) is about Roy Calvert, who appeared as a boy in *Strangers And Brothers*,[1] and who is now a young graduate of the Cambridge College of which Lewis Eliot, when the story begins in 1935, has been a Fellow for about a year.[2] He is the most gifted man that the College has produced for many years past. Already, at twenty-five, he has won an international reputation as an Orientalist—his particular line is deciphering and interpreting fragments of ancient texts. He is extremely handsome and attractive: he is gay and humorous: everything he does, or so it seems, is done with elegance and ease. The Master makes him his protégé. The Master's daughter falls in love with him. Yet in the background there are continual rumours about an extraordinary and tormented private life: drink, women, wild dissipation—it is not a side the College sees, but somehow the College knows. The rumours are true.

Lewis, in the depths of his despair over Sheila, is drawn to Roy, and with insight sharpened by his own suffering, pierces to the secret of Roy's misery. It is no accident, he

[1] He was the unwitting cause of the minor scandal from which George Passant defended Jack Cotery. He is a cousin of Lewis's wife, Sheila.

[2] Lewis's election to a Fellowship is an event which Snow has seen fit, deliberately and tantalisingly, not to recount directly: we are told that it resulted from the activities of Katherine March's husband, Francis Getliffe.

feels, that Roy has chosen to devote himself to restoring texts relating to the Manichæan heresy, a religion in which Man's spirit is part of the light and his flesh part of the dark: the battle sways from side to side—'the most subtle and complex representation of sexual guilt', Lewis comments. Roy in his own life mirrors this struggle between the light and the dark.

But the source of the struggle, Lewis discovers, lies in the depths of Roy's temperament: he is prey to inescapable melancholia. As he fights against it, he fluctuates between a sparkling, energetic composure and a black, hopeless lethargy, from which he can only liberate himself by some act of maniac wildness, usually of a self-destructive nature. Lewis comes to inderstand Roy's temperament before he himself does, realising that the cyclical fluctuation between high spirits and complete despair, with a destructive act as the releasing mechanism, will go on as long as he lives. Time after time, in crisis after crisis, Lewis tries to mitigate the misery and shield his friend from the consequences of the outbursts. All the time his fear is growing; that one day Roy will see the truth clearly and kill himself.

Against the background of European events leading to the Second World War, Lewis watches Roy trying to escape from himself by seeking for some kind of outer authority; seeking it through trying to believe in God, through an extraordinary flirtation with the Nazis in Berlin, through a commonplace marriage to a shallow, attractive girl who will not seek to know him too deeply. All these things fail him. He gives up his war-time job in Intelligence and becomes a bomber pilot because Lewis, Lewis of all people, has let him know that at this stage of the war a bomber pilot stands the highest statistical chance of being killed.

It is a sombre story: paradoxically the effect of the book is not sombre at all, because it is constantly lit up by the bright and flashing aspect of Roy Calvert, the most hero-like, the most romantic of all Snow's figures.

This novel, which is for some readers, because of its attractive and vivid surface, the most haunting and the most 'easy' book of the sequence, has nevertheless a central 'difficulty' the converse of the first novel's. George Passant is sometimes found hard to comprehend and appreciate because he is drawn in exceptional depth and complexity: though Roy Calvert dominates this book and shines over it, too much about him is left untold and unguessable.

The Masters (1951) is the story not of one man but of a group of men—the Fellows of Lewis's Cambridge College, engaged during the year 1937 in electing a new Master. Although there are only thirteen Fellows involved, thirteen academic persons locked away in an ancient institution, the novel is about men's love of power and their equivocal needs to indulge and subdue it. Throughout the rituals of the dining hall and the combination room, the colloguings in seventeenth-century rooms, the to-ings-and-fro-ings across cobbled courts, runs the motive force of political intrigue, as urgent and unassuageable as anywhere in the macrocosm outside.

Although every man plays an individual rôle as an elector, there are three men who are the prime movers in the story —Brown, Chrystal and Jago. Jago is one of the candidates for the Mastership, the other two are the main persons in his supporting caucus. Chrystal, the Dean, is the typical man of power, active and masterful, loving the feel of power— and given to near-adoration for men who win his respect. Yet it is Brown, the apparently contented harmonious fat man, who really dominates the proceedings: tactful, adroit, sensitive to shades of feeling and of mood, fluid yet stable, tolerant, unhurried and outwardly benign, he is the born politician. Brown has chosen Jago, and he draws his friend Chrystal in with him. His task is not easy because Jago is an unusual man. In fact it is the unusual things about him, which sometimes put people off, which appeal to the side of Arthur Brown that is hidden; Jago's impulsiveness, his quick temper, his passionate pride and remorse, his insight and his frankness, in particular his 'nakedness to life'—they are things which Arthur Brown has envied or things in his own nature which he has by force of will had to subjugate.

The alternative candidate is a scientist named Crawford, an able man, an excellent administrator, a successful participant in scientific affairs, bland, impassive, conceited—and impersonal. His supporting caucus is run by Francis Getliffe, also a scientist, who regards him as the candidate any reasonable man would vote for.

In January the Fellows have had the news that the old Master is dying: in December the thirteen men enter the College chapel to elect one of their number Master. The new Master is elected by a majority of seven to six. After months have been spent in discussion and caucus-forming, the one who turns the scale has changed sides during the last twenty-four hours.

The Masters is the most 'comfortable' novel in the sequence. The singleness and the familiarness of the theme give the reader something comparatively easy to catch on to. At the same time the framework of events imposes a unity of time, place and cast of characters as integral as that of, say, *Death Under Sail*. And also the book abounds with those touches of apparently inessential detail which were missing from *Strangers And Brothers*, which here, selected and handled consummately, evoke a friendly, almost cosy warmth.

The New Men (1954) is about the emergence of atomic scientists into the affairs of the nation between 1939 and 1945. Lewis Eliot tells the story of a group of atomic scientists who are working in a government research establishment especially created for them at a place in Warwickshire, called Barford.[1]

At the beginning of the war Lewis, like many other

[1] Though Barford exists as a village in Warwickshire, there was no counterpart to the research establishment in real life. The most talented atomic scientists in this country were sent over to North America to join in the American and Canadian atomic energy projects.

dons, has gone into the Civil Service, and through chance personal connections he is posted to a department of government that is very small, but close to the scientific conduct of the war. It is his Minister, with whom Lewis works intimately, who is entrusted with the task of getting Barford going and keeping an eye on what becomes of it. Thus Lewis sees from the outside how, from the pre-war discovery of nuclear fission, the scientists of Barford move step by step, as purely professional men, to the manufacture of an atomic bomb: he also sees, because one of the scientists is his brother, Martin, their affairs from the inside—he sees them move, in their moral outlook, step by step from optimism and single-mindedness to violent agitation and remorse. The new men start out with the moral responsibility of scientists—a moral responsibility to scientific truth and nothing else. They end at variance with each other and with their own consciences: when they learn that, against their wishes, the bomb has been dropped on Hiroshima, they discover a moral responsibility towards the rest of mankind. The new men have emerged into the world of power and they are confronted with the price they have to pay for it.

These are the events through which Lewis lives, yet, at the heart of *The New Men* there is a second theme. It is an exploration of brotherly love.

In 1939 Martin is at Lewis's College, doing nuclear research, and Lewis induces him to ask—for what to Lewis appears as Martin's own good—to be posted to Barford. Lewis has to do it subtly, because Martin himself is a cautious, subtle young man, far-sighted and calculating, hiding his own romantic hopes under a kind of stoicism. Thus begins the interplay of wills and possessive love between the two brothers. At Barford, set on the track by Lewis, Martin makes the moves necessary for getting on, first by attaching himself to Luke, a better scientist than himself, and finally putting himself in a position—through breaking down a Communist at Barford whom Luke had

decided not to investigate—to profit by Luke's mistake and
to get offered the Chief Superintendency of the establishment. His final moves are not Lewis's moves for him, and
Lewis is shocked, even repelled. They quarrel bitterly. Only
when Martin makes his last throw does Lewis fully realise
that Martin's moves are also moves in assertion of inde-
pendence, of freedom from Lewis's planning for him.

As between Mr. March and Charles, between Lewis's
own mother and himself, the interplay of wills and possessive love can end only in conflict of the one and destruction
of the other. Martin's last throw makes it plain that he has
changed from a younger brother to an independent man.
Lewis knows well enough the fate of filial love by now.

'At the springs of my nature I had some kind of pride or
vanity which not only made me careless of myself but also
prevented me going into the deepest human relation on
equal terms.' That is how Lewis Eliot states his cardinal
discovery about his own nature when, at the beginning of
Homecomings (1957), he takes up again his own life-story
two years after the point where he left off, at the end of
Time Of Hope.

This novel takes Lewis from 1938 to 1948. At the beginning he is still a Cambridge don, and he has added to his
professional activities by becoming a consultant to an
eminent industrialist. Yet his marriage to Sheila, at the core
of his existence, makes his existence sterile. The suffering
she caused him, which, though he despised it, at least
broke down the bar of vanity to his heart, has lost its power.
And Sheila has deteriorated still further: she has even given
up the bursts of cruelty which once brought her feelings to
life.

Yet, though Lewis feels only sorry for her, he is still,
as he always was, apprehensive of what he may find when
he goes home to her. In an atmosphere of growing coldness
and dread, she spends most of her time alone. Then one
day he is called home to her, to find that she has been able
to bear it no longer. She has killed herself. Stricken with

sorrow and remorse, Lewis realises that he is freed. He is
freed to try and find a second, true love: he is freed to *try*
to overcome the flaw at the springs of his own nature.

Numbly he spends a year—the war has now begun—
concentrating on his work as a civil servant in Whitehall:
and then he meets Margaret Davidson. She is a girl of
twenty-four, clever and strong-minded, daughter of a
Bloomsbury family, and also a civil servant. She is attractive, piquantly shy and careless. Lewis is drawn to her
immediately; and she is drawn to him. Her natural insight
into people's natures happens to be sharpest and deepest at
just such places as the one where Lewis's flaw is hidden.
They recognise each other, and she comprehends, as soon
as he tells her about Sheila, the moral struggle of which he
stands on the verge. They fall in love, become lovers, and
then find that to achieve true love a desolating battle lies
ahead of them.

While Lewis becomes steadily more successful in Whitehall,[1] playing an increasing part in the inner workings of the
world of power,[2] his struggle to bring himself into the
kind of relationship with Margaret that will satisfy him
morally swings to and fro. At one point, realising that
Lewis is refusing her his confidence—he has concealed
from her that Sheila's death was suicide—she decides she
in unable to sustain a one-sided relationship in which she
offers trust totally and Lewis offers nothing. She gives up
and marries someone else.

Lewis finds no consolation. When they meet some years
later they find their love for each other has not changed.
Margaret now acts differently. Partly because she is, in
love, completely committed to him; and partly because
love, for her, is linked with moral striving, she gets a

[1] He is able to bring in George Passant as his assistant. It is interesting
to note that while in the first novel George was a 'difficult' character
strange and hard to understand, the latent effect of the earlier book makes
him come up now with the familiarness of an old friend.

[2] Among all the 'external' scenes in the sequence, those set in official
life rank very high.

28 C. P. SNOW

divorce and marries him. Lewis realises now that the
stronger moral impulse cannot come from her: it must
come from himself.

Homecomings ends with Lewis finding that stronger
impulse in himself. Their child, whom Lewis loves without
contraint, falls desperately ill, and he discovers that in his
anguish he is shutting Margaret out. At last he sees how to
reduce the bar from his heart. He longs to go alone to see
his child, but triumphantly he cries to Margaret—and his
tone tells her what depths in his nature the cry comes from
—'Come with me!' The book ends with them coming home.

The setting of *The Affair* is the same as that of *The
Masters*, this time the year being 1953. The story relates how
the Fellows of the College deal with the situation in which
one of their number, a young physicist called Howard, is
accused of scientific fraud. Lewis Eliot is drawn into the
affair firstly, when his brother Martin, who has returned
to the College after resigning from Barford (*The New
Men*), asks his advice privately, and later when he is called
in to act professionally in the legal complications which arise.

In sixteen years the College has changed a good deal.
In particular it has lost some of its inbred air: it has grown
in size, and correspondingly in impersonality; and the
activities of the Fellows outside academic life are beginning
to integrate College affairs with those of the external world.
The cosiness is gone. Arthur Brown, still running the
College—since running the College is what he loves most,
he has come to terms with Crawford, the new Master—
still gives little claret-parties in his rooms for his friends,
where they talk over their plans; yet somehow there is a
feeling that the best days are over. After these meetings the
young Fellows go home and take heed of what their wives
have to say. Willy-nilly College life has acquired more than
a tinge of life at some such place as Barford.

While *The Masters* was a study in politics, *The Affair* is a
study in justice, actually justice tied down and regulated
by a 'fine-structure' of politics, again with the College

microcosm symbolising the macrocosm. Before the story begins, Howard's case has already been considered by a Court composed of the four senior members of the College —the Master, Brown, Nightingale and Winslow. He has been found guilty and ejected from the College. But further evidence is brought to light by another young scientist, no friend of Howard's, which indicates that the first judgement may have been wrong, that what appears to be a fraud may have been committed by Howard's senior colleague, a most distinguished scientist who is now dead. Howard may have been misjudged; yet there is strong resistance among the Fellows to re-opening his case, partly because of renewing the possibility of public scandal, but mostly because Howard is a cold-natured young roughneck with near-Communist opinions.

In the set-up as a whole there is a marked resemblance, as one of the Fellows remarks, to that of the Dreyfus case. (This is why the novel is called *The Affair*.) After much argument and heart-searching, a majority of Fellows demands that the case shall be re-opened. The Court of Seniors duly reaches the same conclusion as before. The majority, unconvinced, now threatens to take the case outside the College. At this, Brown and his party agree to a hearing with legal advisers—Lewis Eliot advises for Howard, whose case now has the support of Martin and of Francis Getliffe—and the last part of the novel is occupied with the legal proceedings.

In the meantime, throughout the novel, there is preparation for the next magisterial election, when Crawford retires, in which the two most likely candidates for the Mastership are Getliffe and Arthur Brown—unless their behaviour over the affair loses them supporters.

At the legal hearing Howard is finally exonerated. But the College resolutely refuses to have him back in more than a token sense.

'The only comfort', observes Crawford, 'is that sensible men usually come to sensible conclusions.'

IV

THEMATIC MATERIAL AND DESIGN

Strangers And Brothers, the title, states at once the deepest theme of the sequence as a whole—that all men, locked away in the isolation of their own selves, are lonely, strangers to each other; while in the similarity and resonance between them, in their joys, their aspirations and their sufferings, they are all brothers. And every man exists in his own dynamic equilibrium between the two, sometimes more stranger than brother, sometimes more brother than stranger.

What are men, solitarily, in themselves? and How, in their common experiences, are they brothers? These are the two main questions which Snow sets out to investigate; experimentally, with techniques like those of a scientist, making hypotheses about the natures of his characters and testing them against the way those characters behave, suggesting theories about how in general their actions arise, yet concerning himself always with individual acts and their causes. And these are the two main questions whose answers, so far as they are to be found, Snow conveys to the reader by means of the techniques of art, adopting a tone of evocation and revelation, so that the reader, as well as being told the answers, *knows* them—he becomes aware that he is a stranger and a brother himself.

Apropos the investigatory element in his work, Snow wrote,[1] in the early days of his career as a writer, that he wanted to examine: 'How much of what we *are* is due to accidents of our class and time, and how much is due to something innate and unalterable within ourselves?'

It is clear that to do this he had to portray the society in which his characters were embedded, and to study the moral and political health of that society. In *Strangers And Brothers* the extent of the society under examination is as

[1] Letter to his publisher, 1938.

broad as Balzac's,[1] ranging from the provincial lower middle-class to cosmopolitan aristocracy: it includes the worlds of government, university and industry. And the period of time will, in the end, encompass half a century. The sounding of the moral and political health of society is generally implicit, made plain to the reader through the behaviour of the characters as seen by Lewis Eliot: for example, the form in which the particular turns of conscience of Charles March and Ann express themselves—for all Charles's and Ann's striving after goodness, a form cruelly destructive—illuminates the defects and decadence of upper-class Anglo-Jewish society in the 1930's.

All the same, where the question is posed in general terms, *Strangers And Brothers* gives the answer that men seem to be *less* what they *are* due to accidents of class and time than to things innate and unalterable within themselves. Lewis Eliot's is a dark view of life. Nevertheless, *Strangers And Brothers* is a novel about individuals grappling with their fate, rather than having it either imposed on them by random external events or imposed on them at birth as a foregone conclusion.[2] The crisis in each book of the sequence is essentially tragic, and yet not unrelievedly tragic; because somehow Snow irradiates it with a belief in the ultimate fortitude of the human race, with a belief that in the acceptance of the essential tragic nature of their own situation men are nevertheless borne up, rightly, by hope for what lies ahead. Their situation is tragic but their fibres are *alive* with hope—this concept is the key to Lewis Eliot's own moral attitude to life.

At the same time the tragic nature of the human situation, as seen by Lewis Eliot, is relieved at levels nearer to the surface. First of all there is a characteristic *down-to-earthness* about the author. For example, the possessive love of

[1] Snow, like Balzac, reveals character against the background of society: but the structure of *Strangers And Brothers*, unlike that of *La Comédie Humaine*, is built upon the underlying personal theme or themes.
[2] This theme of constant struggle gives dramatic suspense throughout the whole sequence beyond narrative suspense in any particular member.

parents for children is a 'darkness of the heart', yet Snow
presents it as so much the lot of all of us that we no more
expect it to break the lives of his characters than it breaks
our own lives. Secondly there is an ironic nerve of comedy
always in play. It is important not to miss this: for example,
at the height of their sufferings, Mr. March is still clowning,
Roy Calvert playing monkey-tricks on pompous people,
Lewis himself being outmanœuvred by his slatternly
landlady. And thirdly, the tragic stories are invested with a
peculiar kind of glamour that springs partly from the
subduedly romantic way in which Lewis, with his 'residue
of identification with those outside, pushing their noses
against the window',[1] sees life—the glamour of midnight
visits of intrigue in a College, of the tormented bohemian
ways of a dazzling scholar, of secret confabulations 'in the
corridors of power'—and partly by the rôle played in
precipitating the crises of the stories by scandal, which
has, in its capacity for drawing everybody cosily and
sensationally in, an alluringness not far removed from
glamour.[2]

The central story of the sequence, the story of Lewis
Eliot, is strong and simple: through it are interwoven the
stories of his friends. The social relationship of the different
characters to each other is intricate; but it is the intricate
relationship of their experience with Lewis's experience,
that enables Snow to build up a novel of remarkable
psychological as well as social solidity. Yet this intricacy
in thematic relationship is not aimed merely at producing
solidity in the architectural sense: its function is to provide
means for the kind of revealing and evoking which is at
the heart of Snow's technique as an artist. The clue to this
function is given in a note written by Snow himself, in
the Prefatory Note to *The Conscience Of The Rich*, about
the design of *Strangers And Brothers*.

[1] *The Affair*, Part II, Chapter XIII.
[2] In the use of scandal, Snow has obviously learned a good deal from
Ibsen.

Obviously, the entire work tells the stories of a number of people through a period of time: that does not need saying. Obviously, through the entire work there is an attempt to give some insights into society: those have been better understood than I expected when I began. Nevertheless, the inner design has always lain elsewhere—at any rate for me, and I cannot speak for anyone else. It consists of a resonance between what Lewis Eliot sees and what he feels. Some of the more important emotional themes he observes through others' experience, and then finds them enter into his own. The theme of possessive love is introduced through Mr. March's relation to his son: this theme reappears in *The New Men* in Lewis's own experience, through his relation to his brother, and again, still more directly, in *Homecomings*.

The clue is: 'It consists of a resonance between what Lewis Eliot sees and what he feels'. Resonance: it is the phenomenon of something that vibrates being able to stir and magnify a similar vibration in something that has been previously *attuned*, which gives *Strangers And Brothers* its power, through evocation and revelation, over one's emotions and one's imagination.

There are resonances of many kinds and on many levels.

Although the sequence is not yet complete, the extent to which the author has planned to use one kind of resonance is fully apparent. For instance, in George Passant's story Lewis observes, among other things, the love of power impelling a man whose character is flawed; in Charles March's story, the love of a parent who wants certain things for his son: in *Time Of Hope* both these themes appear, resonating in Lewis's own experience. There is some similarity, in this use of resonance, with *A La Recherche du Temps Perdu*, where Proust examines the theme of obsessional jealousy in Swann, before coming to it in Marcel. What Snow does is to extend it in a *cyclical* fashion. This is original: no other writer has done it. The first two novels are about what Lewis sees; *Time Of Hope* about what he feels during the period of the first two: the next three are about what he sees, *Homecomings* about what he feels:

the cycle has been gone through twice, in the second
round with a wider range of observations and a greater
depth of experience. During the first cycle there is a resonance between what Lewis has seen and what he feels:
during the second there is a similar resonance within the
cycle, and also a resonance between the second cycle and
the first—the effect is cumulative. And it is evident that a
third cycle will be added, touching off still wider internal
resonances, to bring the sequence to an end.

V

STYLE

I answered sullenly. The present moment, the existent moment —as we sat there, in the sultry darkness, we could neither deal with it nor let it be. We could not show each other the kindness we should have shown strangers: far less could we allow those words to come out which, with the knowledge and touch of intimacy, we were certain could give the other a night's peace. If she could have said to me, it doesn't matter, leave it, some day you'll be better and we'll start again—if I could have said to her, I will try to give you all you want, marry me and somehow we shall come through—But we could not speak so, it was as though our throats were sewn up.

We stayed, our hands touching, not tired so much as stupefied while the time passed: time not racing hallucinatorily by, as when one is drunk, but just pressing on us with something like the headaching pressure of the thundery air in which we sat. Sometimes we talked, almost with interest, almost as though we were going out for the first time, for the first meal together, about a play that ought to be seen or a book she had just read. After another bout of silence, she said in a different tone: 'Before we started I asked what you wanted from me.' *Homecomings*, Ch. XXVI.

Two things strike one immediately: the first, how simple the literary style appears to be; the second, how much, in a matter of 230 words, happens to have been said. The two things are directly related. The words chosen are those which say most.

For the most important and serious things he has to say in this passage, Snow has chosen to write mainly in simple common words,[1] words that we all use all of the time—, especially at moments when we are struggling to express something difficult. His underlying aesthetic theory is clear. The simple common words, because we use them all the time, often using the same word for different purposes,

[1] Over 80 per cent of the words are monosyllables. Less than 15 per cent have two syllables; and less than 4 per cent have three or more.

are the words which have come to acquire separately the most elaborate nexus of allusions;[1] and therefore, strung together they can make the most subtle and pregnant of sentences. Furthermore, because they are simple and common, they do not distract in a 'literary' sense: because they are familiar, one feels naked to their meaning. 'If I could have said to her, I will try to give you all you want, marry me and somehow we shall come through'—that is how, in this complex situation of conflicting love, one might have said it to oneself: reading it, nothing comes between one and the author's meaning. The style has fitted perfectly what the author had to say.

While appearing simple, the style is, of course, strong and subtly poetic. (Snow relies little on adverbs—there are only two in the above passage.) Common words are interspersed with uncommon ones, carefully chosen for their effect on more than one level—e.g. in the first two lines 'sullen' and 'sultry' ring on a poetic level, and in so doing they bind together more strongly the mood of the characters with the atmosphere of the place in which they are sitting. Polysyllabic words, when they are used, make their special impression—e.g. in the third sentence, 'intimacy' stands out: struck by it, one remembers the characters have been intimate as lovers. Even more markedly, Snow makes the most of literary images—e.g. at the end of the last sentence of the first paragraph, the tension built up by the sentences linked with dashes is clinched, as it could not have been clinched by the statement 'But we could not speak so', by the remarkable image, 'it was as though our throats were sewn up'.

To illustrate Snow's total range in verbal texture, one has to go further than one extract. It is significant that Snow varies his verbal texture according to what he is writing about. In general, he presents scene and narrative most simply. For comment, especially the kind of extended

[1] Compare the nexus of allusions associated respectively with the words 'give' and 'hallucinatorily'.

comment with which he sometimes ends a chapter, his verbal texture usually becomes denser, richer, more elaborate. For example:—

> As to many of us, when young, the labile, the shifting, the ambivalent, the Lebedevs and Fyodor Karamazovs, had given me an intimation of the depth and wonder of life. *Homecomings*, Ch. XXVIII.

Both structurally and syntactically, Snow's style is also more complex and more calculated than it seems. For example, the second paragraph of the longer quotation is constructed to lead suspensefully from the static 'We stayed, our hands touching', through the disturbing 'head-aching pressure of the thundery air', the desultory strain of 'Sometimes we talked, almost with interest', to the climax of what it was that she said in a different tone.

But the main point about Snow's style is that it has been developed firstly to give *absolute conviction on the plane of immediate fact*, though it has been developed so flexibly that it can also be used for both motive and analytical purposes. It has a compelling tone which arises not only, or even mainly, from knowledge, but from the author's total involvement in what he is doing. To read it is to believe it. The fact that Snow has such a wide experience and under-standing of life in England naturally gives what he writes a peculiar authority: his style, simple, unaffected and moving is such as to make what he writes immediately recognisable as plain truth.

VI

BASIC ATTITUDE

When Snow expresses his view on what is happening nowadays in the world in general, two main theses are discernible. The first arises from his concern over the widening, in the Western world, of the gap between science and literature: his thesis is that this widening is in any case intellectually and socially undesirable; and that in the case of a country in the particular situation that ours is in, it could in a short time be catastrophic. He argues that the splintering of a culture into an increasing number of fragments, between which communication becomes less and less possible, inevitably leads to attrition and decay. A country as small as ours cannot afford fragmentation of any kind. Our economic future depends on our keeping ahead in technological innovation; and any split which hives off part of our intellectual and social potential into non-comprehension of, if not opposition to, scientific studies and activities, is likely to be disastrous that much more quickly than it would be for a larger, richer country which is not compelled to make absolutely the most of its available talent.

The second thesis is that the widening of the gap between science and literature in the Western world obscures the existence of the major gap in the whole world today, namely that between the countries which are technologically advanced and the rest—major because it is a more deep-seated cause of possible world conflict than any other. The prime social task of the advanced countries, for the sake of their own continued peaceful existence if no one else's, is to reduce the gap. This can only be done by helping the less advanced countries to industrialise themselves as rapidly as possible. And this in turn can only be done if the advanced countries are confident in their own culture— i.e. are confident in the results of their own industrialisation.

The split in Western culture between the scientific and the non-scientific parts has its root superficially in the incapacity of the non-scientific part to comprehend the scientific; but more deeply in the incapacity of the non-scientific part to adjust itself to—let alone have confidence in—the conditions of life in industrialised society. Before the potentially tragic consequences of the culture's being so divided, Snow's attitude is the reverse of acquiescent. In this, as well as in his novels, he is totally involved. '*Though the individual condition is tragic, the social condition need not be.*' Lewis Eliot's view of human nature is a dark one, yet some things in the tragic human condition can be affected, as his own condition is affected in *Time Of Hope* and more particularly *Homecomings*, by the exercise of will; and this gives him hope. So Snow views what is happening nowadays in the world in general. The split in the culture alarms him; and the gap between the rich advanced nations and the poverty-stricken backward ones troubles him both practically and morally. But both gaps can be reduced by men of good-will if they set themselves out to do it. There is no reason why the human *social* condition should be tragic. It can be affected by human action. There *is* hope for the future.

C. P. SNOW
A Select Bibliography

(Place of publication London, unless stated otherwise)

Scientific Papers:

PROCEEDINGS OF THE ROYAL SOCIETY, 1928–9, 30–32, 35
—papers on molecular structure.

Separate Works:

DEATH UNDER SAIL (1932)
—revised and reprinted 1959.
NEW LIVES FOR OLD (1933).
THE SEARCH (1934)
—revised and reprinted 1958.
STRANGERS AND BROTHERS (1940).
THE LIGHT AND THE DARK (1947).
TIME OF HOPE (1949).
THE MASTERS (1951).
THE NEW MEN (1954).
HOMECOMINGS (1956).
THE CONSCIENCE OF THE RICH (1958).
THE AFFAIR (1960).
TWO CULTURES AND THE SCIENTIFIC REVOLUTION. Cambridge (1959)
—the Rede Lecture at Cambridge, 1959.
SCIENCE AND GOVERNMENT Oxford (1961)
—the Godkin Lecture.

Some Critical Studies:

THREE NOVELISTS AND THE DRAWING OF CHARACTER, by Pamela Hansford
  Johnson
—in English Studies, 1950.
THE NOVEL, by Walter Allen (1955).
READING A NOVEL, by Walter Allen (1950)
—essay on *The Masters*.

THE NOVEL, LIVING OR DEAD—A GATHERING OF FUGITIVES, by Lionel
  Trilling (1957).

———————————

C. P. Snow's novels are published by Messrs. Macmillan.

WRITERS AND THEIR WORK

General Editor: BONAMY DOBRÉE

The first 55 issues in the Series appeared under the General Editorship of T. O. BEACHCROFT

Sixteenth Century and Earlier:
FRANCIS BACON: J. Max Patrick
CHAUCER: Nevill Coghill
ENGLISH MARITIME WRITING:
　Hakluyt to Cook: Oliver Warner
MALORY: M. C. Bradbrook
MARLOWE: Philip Henderson
SIDNEY: Kenneth Muir
SKELTON: Peter Green
SPENSER: Rosemary Freeman
WYATT: Sergio Baldi

Seventeenth Century:
SIR THOMAS BROWNE: Peter Green
BUNYAN: Henri Talon
CAVALIER POETS: Robin Skelton
DONNE: Frank Kermode
DRYDEN: Bonamy Dobrée
HERRICK: John Press
HOBBES: T. E. Jessop
BEN JONSON: J. B. Bamborough
LOCKE: Maurice Cranston
ANDREW MARVELL: John Press
MILTON: E. M. W. Tillyard
SHAKESPEARE: C. J. Sisson
SHAKESPEARE:
　CHRONICLES: Clifford Leach
　EARLY COMEDIES: Derek Traversi
　GREAT TRAGEDIES: Kenneth Muir
　LATE COMEDIES: G. K. Hunter
　PROBLEM PLAYS: Peter Ure
THREE METAPHYSICAL POETS:
　　　　Margaret Willy
IZAAK WALTON: Margaret Bottrall

Eighteenth Century:
BERKELEY: T. E. Jessop
BLAKE: Kathleen Raine
BOSWELL: P. A. W. Collins
BURKE: T. E. Utley
BURNS: David Daiches
COWPER: N. Nicholson
CRABBE: R. L. Brett
DEFOE: J. R. Sutherland

ENGLISH HYMNS: Arthur Pollard
FIELDING: John Butt
GIBBON: C. V. Wedgwood
GOLDSMITH: A. Norman Jeffares
GRAY: R. W. Ketton-Cremer
JOHNSON: S. C. Roberts
POPE: Ian Jack
RICHARDSON: R. F. Brissenden
SHERIDAN: W. A. Darlington
CHRISTOPHER SMART:
　　　　Geoffrey Grigson
SMOLLETT: Laurence Brander
STEELE, ADDISON AND THEIR
　PERIODICAL ESSAYS:
　　　　A. R. Humphreys
STERNE: D. W. Jefferson
SWIFT: J. Middleton Murry
HORACE WALPOLE: Hugh Honour

Nineteenth Century:
MATTHEW ARNOLD: Kenneth Allott
JANE AUSTEN: S. Townsend Warner
THE BRONTE SISTERS:
　　　　Phyllis Bentley
BROWNING: John Bryson
SAMUEL BUTLER: G. D. H. Cole
BYRON: Herbert Read
CARLYLE: David Gascoyne
LEWIS CARROLL: Derek Hudson
COLERIDGE: Kathleen Raine
DICKENS: K. J. Fielding
DISRAELI: Paul Bloomfield
GEORGE ELIOT: Lettice Cooper
ENGLISH TRAVELLERS IN THE NEAR
　EAST: Robin Fedden
FITZGERALD: Joanna Richardson
MRS. GASKELL: Miriam Allott
GISSING: A. C. Ward
THOMAS HARDY: R. A. Scott-James
HAZLITT: J. B. Priestley
G. M. HOPKINS: Geoffrey Grigson
T. H. HUXLEY: William Irvine
KEATS: Edmund Blunden
LAMB: Edmund Blunden

LANDOR: G. Rostrevor Hamilton
MACAULAY: G. R. Potter
JOHN STUART MILL: M. Cranston
WILLIAM MORRIS: P. Henderson
NEWMAN: J. M. Cameron
PATER: Iain Fletcher
ROSSETTI: Oswald Doughty
RUSKIN: Peter Quennell
SIR WALTER SCOTT: Ian Jack
SHELLEY: Stephen Spender
R. L. STEVENSON: G. B. Stern
SWINBURNE: H. J. C. Grierson
TENNYSON: F. L. Lucas
THACKERAY: Laurence Brander
FRANCIS THOMPSON: P. Butter
TROLLOPE: Hugh Sykes Davies
OSCAR WILDE: James Laver
WORDSWORTH: Helen Darbishire

Twentieth Century:
W. H. AUDEN: Richard Hoggart
HILAIRE BELLOC: Renée Haynes
ARNOLD BENNETT: F. Swinnerton
EDMUND BLUNDEN: Alec M. Hardie
ELIZABETH BOWEN: Jocelyn Brooke
ROY CAMPBELL: David Wright
JOYCE CARY: Walter Allen
G. K. CHESTERTON: C. Hollis
WINSTON CHURCHILL: John Connell
R. G. COLLINGWOOD:
E. W. F. Tomlin
I. COMPTON-BURNETT:
Pamela Hansford Johnson
JOSEPH CONRAD: Oliver Warner
WALTER DE LA MARE: K. Hopkins
THE DETECTIVE STORY IN
BRITAIN: Julian Symons
NORMAN DOUGLAS: Ian Greenlees
T. S. ELIOT: M. C. Bradbrook
FORD MADOX FORD: Kenneth Young
E. M. FORSTER: Rex Warner

CHRISTOPHER FRY: Derek Stanford
JOHN GALSWORTHY: R. H. Mottram
ROBERT GRAVES: M. Seymour Smith
GRAHAM GREENE: Francis Wyndham
L. P. HARTLEY and ANTHONY POW-
ELL: P. Bloomfield and B. Bergonzi
A. E. HOUSMAN: Ian Scott-Kilvert
ALDOUS HUXLEY: Jocelyn Brooke
HENRY JAMES: Michael Swan
JAMES JOYCE: J. I. M. Stewart
RUDYARD KIPLING: B. Dobrée
D. H. LAWRENCE: Kenneth Young
C. DAY LEWIS: Clifford Dyment
WYNDHAM LEWIS: E. W. F. Tomlin
KATHERINE MANSFIELD: Ian Gordon
JOHN MASEFIELD: L. A. G. Strong
SOMERSET MAUGHAM: J. Brophy
EDWIN MUIR: J. C. Hall
J. MIDDLETON MURRY: Philip Mairet
GEORGE ORWELL: Tom Hopkinson
POETS OF THE 1939-45 WAR:
R. N. Currey
J. B. PRIESTLEY: Ivor Brown
HERBERT READ: Francis Berry
BERTRAND RUSSELL: Alan Dorward
BERNARD SHAW: A. C. Ward
EDITH SITWELL: John Lehmann
OSBERT SITWELL: Roger Fulford
C. P. SNOW: William Cooper
LYTTON STRACHEY:
R. A. Scott-James
DYLAN THOMAS: G. S. Fraser
G. M. TREVELYAN: J. H. Plumb
WAR POETS: 1914-18:
Edmund Blunden
EVELYN WAUGH: Christopher Hollis
H. G. WELLS: Montgomery Belgion
CHARLES WILLIAMS:
John Heath-Stubbs
VIRGINIA WOOLF: Bernard Blackstone
W. B. YEATS: G. S. Fraser

In Preparation:

MEREDITH: Phyllis Bartlett
J. M. SYNGE and LADY GREGORY:
Elizabeth Coxhead

THE POWYS BROTHERS:
R. C. Churchill
RONALD FIRBANK and JOHN
BETJEMAN: Jocelyn Brooke